eric mendelsohn

by Wolf Von Eckardt

DISTRIBUTED BY POCKET BOOKS, INC.

George Braziller, Inc.
NEW YORK, 1960

This book is dedicated to

MRS. LOUISE MENDELSOHN

whose perceptive enthusiasm has contributed as much to it as the factual and illustrative material she has so generously made available.

ACKNOWLEDGMENTS

Hans J. Schiller; Richard Neutra, FAIA; Percival Good-man, FAIA; and Richard M. Bennett, AIA, have been of great help in sharing their recollections of Eric Mendelsohn with me.

I am also indebted to Mrs. Gudrun Huden for tracking down hard-to-find references; to Mrs. Betty Robinson for struggling with my syntax and punctuation; and to Mr. Carl Feiss, AIA, AIP, for his valuable comments on the manuscript.

CONTENTS

"The truly creative artist has faith in his time."

—RICHARD LIPPOLD

1. FANTASIES REALIZED

IT WAS THE uneasy spring of 1919. Eric Mendelsohn had just returned from the war and was eager to resume his architectural practice. To make himself known, he decided to exhibit some of the flamboyant fantasies he had sketched in the trenches—visions of buildings of a kind no one had seen before. He had them redrawn as bold, black posters and called them "Architecture in Steel and Concrete." The critics, however, saw in them little more than imaginative vignettes, amusing, perhaps, as book illustrations.

Just before the exhibition opened at the famous avant-garde art gallery of Paul Cassirer in Berlin, the architect's wife was contemplating these drawings in silence. Her meditation was jolted when Cassirer said: "Tell your husband to take another road. He will never be able to realize such fantastic structures!" Mrs. Mendelsohn found it hard to control herself. All she said was: "He will!"

And he did.

The exhibition was not a success. But the following year an exciting new building went up near Potsdam which catapulted the unknown young Mendelsohn to immediate fame—the Einstein Tower, an observatory and astro-physical laboratory (plates 1, 4–6). It was an entirely novel structure, reminiscent at once of Gaudí's bizarre *art nouveau* architecture of some fifteen years earlier and of Le Corbusier's triumph of architectural sculpture at Ronchamp some thirty-six years later—a Mendelsohn fantasy realized.

That same year Mendelsohn also designed a steel-and-glass hall for a hat factory in Luckenwalde, near Berlin, which is as squarely "modern," as "radiant and naked," as any of the early "functional" architecture. Soon thereafter he replaced this hall with a completely new plant, built in concrete, which, according to Henry-Russell Hitchcock, was "rightly recognized as one of the signal productions of those crucial years in the early twenties when the concepts of the new architecture were first tentatively recognized . . ."[1] (plates 7–10).

Mendelsohn himself, thirty years later, could not fully explain the design of the Einstein Tower. It was a product of "the mystique around Einstein's universe," he said. But Luckenwalde, he continued, was the result of "the clear-cut facts of industry . . . a building which in its use, structure, and shape is clearly intelli-

Sketch for Railway Terminal, 1914

Sketch for Factory of Steel, 1914

Sketch for Motor Car Chassis Factory, 1914

gible. Between these two poles—the rational and the irrational—moves my nature, life, and work."[2]

Mendelsohn's creative spark was ignited in World War I, like that of the other masters of world architecture of his generation. A civilization, it seemed to them, was at the end of its wits. They were determined to bring about a new beginning. Inspired by the revolution in the fine arts and by the vanguard of modern architecture—Perret, Garnier, van de Velde, the early Frank Lloyd Wright, and others—Gropius drafted his first Bauhaus proclamation on the battlefield of Namur; Mies van der Rohe designed his first glass structure as soon as he got out of uniform; Le Corbusier developed his architectural theory during a wartime teaching job; and Mendelsohn sketched his architectural visions while on guard duty in the trenches. "As few before us," he said, "we felt the meaning of living and dying, of end and beginning—its creative meaning in the midst of the silent terror of no-man's land and the terrifying din of rapid fire."[3]

But while Gropius, Mies, and Le Corbusier sought to create new forms for a new civilization out of their rational interpretation of the needs of the time and the dictates of a new technology, Mendelsohn was guided by his artistic intuition.

Tracing paper was scarce at the front and most of his sketches are tiny, although they often depict structures of large scale. All of them are, in his words, "skirted by one contour—bulging, protruding and retracting—suggesting the elastic tension of the steel and concrete structure, and, to be sure, the young architect's mental tension as well!"[4] There is endless variety in their forms and shapes, but this contour, this flow of continuity, which gives unity to even the more intricate design, remains a common characteristic. Another is the rhythm, the well-composed repetition, of alternating sequences. These first sketches, he said later, offer "the clue to everything that follows. For when the first idea is deep enough, life is too short to expound it fully."[5]

His first sketches were, indeed, the clue to everything that follows. Once Mendelsohn had all the facts about the site and the purpose of a building, his design was not a studious search for form that would follow function but, as his assistant Hans Schiller has put it, one short moment of intense concentration until his soft, 6B pencil touched the sketch book. Then came the "outflowing of inspired imagination." It was "the criterion against which he would check all future development of the project, his own variations on the theme, and the elaborations of those who translated its portents into working drawings. 'Look at my sketch,' he would say. 'There is everything in it.' "[6]

Yet intuitive design was always balanced by the other pole—the rational. Mendelsohn agreed with Gropius, Mies, and Le Corbusier that "certainly, the primary element in architecture is function." But "function without sensibility remains mere construction," he added. "If the rationalist's blood does not freeze, and mere imagination goes a step further towards ratio, then they may unite. Otherwise both will be destroyed—the functionalist by a deadly chill in his veins, the dynamicist by the heat of his own fire. Thus, function plus dynamics is the challenge!"[7]

Sketch for Water Tower, 1917

Sketch for Optical Factory, 1917

Sketch for Industrial Complex, 1914

Gropius, in 1910, pioneered the curtain wall, now a basic feature of the International Style, by setting the vertical supports of his Fagus works back to achieve the aesthetic effect of an unbroken glass façade. Mendelsohn, in his Herpich store in Berlin of 1924 (plate 15) and his later Schocken department stores built in 1926 to 1928 (plates 16–20), pushed the structural framework even further back to create an uninterrupted shop window on the ground floor and continuous, well-lit sales counters on the floors above. His Columbus House (plates 32–34), also in Berlin, was, in 1929, probably the first large office building in which the interior space is unobstructed so that the needs of each new tenant can be met with temporary partitions. Mies created such open and flexible interiors much later. Today this means of adding to the rental value has become the major justification for the sterile, "functional" design of glass-box office buildings.

Nor was structure of less interest to Mendelsohn than to his peers. The reinforced-concrete framework of the Luckenwalde factory, the extreme cantilevers of the Schocken stores, the concrete dome of his Cleveland synagogue (plates 85–88), and the Maimonides Hospital (plates 73–74) are examples of imaginative engineering. But Mendelsohn did not construct his architecture; he conceived it *in toto* and then demanded of engineers that they help him realize his structural ideas. Once, Hans Schiller recalls, he adamantly insisted on a "curtain of light" for one of his synagogues. No crash program could have been more intensive than the ensuing frenzy of experimental research, which involved most of his staff. It would have been relatively simple, of course, to contain light in the reflecting particles of well-directed smoke. But Mendelsohn did not want incense. He wanted a clean, unscented "curtain of light, damn it!" It's a pity he never got it.

Mendelsohn passionately envisioned a *new* architecture as fervently as the rest of the moderns. With Gropius, Mies, Poelzig, Bruno and Max Taut, and Ernst May, among others, he organized an architectural action group, the "Ring," in the early twenties, to fight for modern architecture against uncomprehending German bureaucrats and a skeptical public. But *his* modern architecture, as envisioned in his early sketches, strove to express and exploit the plastic, or, as he called it, "elastic" potential of steel and reinforced concrete. In that potential he saw huge spans and cantilevers and new, sculptural forms in the organic image of nature rather than the geometric pedantry of man. As he pointed out shortly before his death in 1953, buildings such as Frank Lloyd Wright's Racine wax factory (1940 and 1950), Nervi's Turin Exhibition Hall (1948), or Torroja's Madrid Hippodrome (1949) are realizations of his prophecy.[8] Today we can name many more free-form structures which vividly recall Mendelsohn's early sketches. Eero Saarinen's airport buildings at Idlewild and at Chantilly, near Washington, D.C., Félix Candela's work in Mexico, or Jorn Utzon's National Opera House for Sidney, Australia, are examples.[9]

But Mendelsohn's actual buildings, too, have in certain ways anticipated a very recent development in modern architecture. We are getting disillusioned, it seems, with the false promise of machine production, its antiseptic monotony, and its pressures towards conformity—and with the architecture which this false promise produced. Mendelsohn's Schocken stores, his Columbus House, his Bexhill Pavilion (plates 43–46), his Maimonides Hospital presage our gradual rediscovery of the value of the individual, of the creative spirit, and of personal self-expression. They point the way from the impersonal to the human, as does much of the more gracious and decorative architecture, often called modern baroque, which we now find in the work of the second generation of the moderns, such as Saarinen, Marcel Breuer, Paul Rudolph, or Minoru Yamasaki. Little, if any, of this architecture existed during Mendelsohn's lifetime.

Like many architects, Mendelsohn was given to occasional flights into wordy and often poetic obfuscation about the meaning and mission of his profession. But he left theorizing and rationalizing to others. "I don't think of theories," he said. "I have my hands full holding my visions, putting them on paper, clarifying them."[10] Attempts to research scientifically or explain the mysteries of artistic creation and development only amused him. S. Giedion's contention in *Space, Time and Architecture*—which inexplicably never once mentions Mendelsohn—that modern art and architecture have discovered time as a new, fourth dimension struck him as ludicrous.[11] He marked the pages which thus extend the Theory of Relativity and sent them, tongue in cheek, to Albert Einstein. The answer was prompt:

"Dear Mr. Mendelsohn,

The passage you sent me from the book *Space, Time and Architecture* has inspired me to the following reply:

It's never hard some new thought to declare
If any nonsense one will dare.
But rarely do you find that novel babble
Is at the same time reasonable.*

Cordially yours, Albert Einstein

P. S.: It is simply bull without any rational basis."[12]

The secret of Mendelsohn's exuberant artistic certainty may well be his great faith in our time and the promise it holds for a better, more beautiful man-made environment. He might well have been bitter. He lost one eye to cancer and the country in which he thrived to Hitler. Three times he had to assert himself in new surroundings—in England, in Palestine, and finally in the United States. But Nazism, a second world war, and his own struggles never altered his belief, expressed in a letter to his wife in 1910, "that a new civilization is beginning, based upon the great conceptions of ancient times."[13] He always looked forward. In

* *Nicht schwer ist's Neues auszusagen*
Wenn jeden Blödsinn man will wagen.
Doch selt'ner füget sich dabei
Dass Neues auch Vernünftig sei!
—Translation above by the author.

14

1951, when such things were still far from the average person's mind, he had his students design interplanetary launching platforms. And he repeatedly stated that he viewed "with profound optimism the wide road of America's architectural future."[14]

"When Bach plays, God goes to the Mass."

—AMÉDÉE OZENFANT

2. *GROWTH OF AN ARTIST*

MENDELSOHN USUALLY PLAYED records while he worked on his designs and this fact soon got around wherever he set up office. It seems almost inevitable, therefore, that one day a young couple timidly asked him to design a house for them —according to Brahms!

Mendelsohn just laughed. He laughed not only because his record player spun Bach records almost exclusively—sometimes the same fugue over and over again —but also because his creative process was at once less romantic and more complex than that. There is, to be sure, an affinity to music in his architecture. In a few of his sketches he did, indeed, consciously or subconsciously translate musical compositions into imaginary structures, into what approximates the poetic definition of architecture as "frozen music." He sketched some lovely designs to Bach's Toccata in C Major and to a Brahms Quintet. But his incessant record playing served not so much his love of music as his need for concentration. It provided a curtain of noise behind which he was shielded from the outside world.

Creating is desperately lonely. Outside interference can be exasperating beyond words. A sculptor's or painter's creation is his own until he gives it to the world. But the architect's creative process is in constant friction with reality—budgets, technical feasibility, the behavior and availability of materials, building codes, and, often most difficult of all, the tastes and foibles of clients and authorities. More often than not, the outcome of this purgatory is mediocrity. Eric Mendelsohn was one of those few architects whose initial creative concept nearly always triumphed. But the process was hectic and tempestuous. And, as with many artists, it required as much of his strength as of his genius. It often made him edgy, contemptuous of others, and seemingly arrogant. He offended many with his ready wit and sharp tongue.

Mendelsohn's office, at the time of his greatest success in Germany, numbered as many as forty assistants and was one of the largest architectural firms in

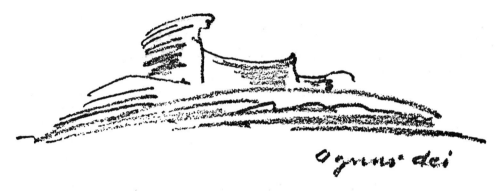

"Agnus Dei," 1921

Europe. He dominated it completely. "There is only one designer here," he would say, "and that is Eric Mendelsohn!" And he did, indeed, design almost everything himself—down to the last detail, doorknob, and drapery. He rarely entrusted his designs to the amplification of landscape architects or of interior decorators, whom he called "interior desecrators." Working with fanatic zeal, he hardly ever took time out for lunch and often had even his dinner brought to the drafting table. He expected the same ardor from his staff and had no use, as he once said, for people who get ulcers. In his perfectionism he would tear out an entire interior wall at his own expense, because a door seemed to him one inch too far to one side. Yet he would think nothing, in a fit of creative rage, of splashing paint all over a laboriously perfected model just before it had to be shipped to the client, in order to try a different color. No wonder none of his associations with other architects lasted long. "When God created the world he had no associates, so why should I?" he scribbled, no doubt facetiously, on a paper Hans Schiller found after his death.

And yet to his friends—and he had many—Eric Mendelsohn was generous, considerate, and affectionate. When the Nazi tide drowned Germany he helped his friends and even the most distant relatives to safe shores. Most of his clients, students, and assistants loved and respected him. And much as he might carry on in the office, many of his employees nostalgically recall the happy comradeship when, deep in the night, the record player would go full blast and Mrs. Mendelsohn would bring coffee and cake to keep the spirits awake.

Mendelsohn met Louise Maas in 1910, when she was sixteen. They married five years later and had one daughter. Mrs. Mendelsohn, a cellist and a woman of unusual charm, culture, and beauty, has devoted her entire life, even beyond his death, to her husband's work and world. "How often on our road through life," she recalls, "would I have loved to hold him back, to warn him of the consequences of his aggressiveness. But I felt almost ashamed to even think of the attempt. Eric's temperament had to take its course, whether it caused him suffer-

16

ing or triumphant laughter. One had no right to change the course his inner force would take him."

Mendelsohn's wife and daughter were undoubtedly an important source of his great inner strength. Another was his happy childhood. He was born in 1887 in the small East Prussian town of Allenstein, now called Olsztyn. His father was a self-made businessman of Russian-Polish background whose industry, altruism, and quest for learning and culture earned him much prestige. His mother devoted herself to music, in addition to raising five children with but modest means for their education, and seems to have been responsible for arousing Mendelsohn's great interest in it.

Mendelsohn loved the open landscape of his childhood. East Prussia is beautiful with its many small lakes, groves of swaying birch trees, and the sweet summer scent of blooming heather. From his bedroom window the boy would watch the play of shadows on the rough masonry texture of the medieval castle of the Teutonic Order which dominates Allenstein. By all accounts he spent most of his time building such castles of clay, sand, or anything he could get hold of.

His father wanted him to study economics and he obliged for a short while, until the lure of Allenstein castle drew him to his real passion—architecture. After a year at the *Technische Hochschule* in Berlin he switched to that in Munich, where he graduated in 1914. He worked his way through architecture school by selling his paintings, decorating store windows, and, with great verve, designing the decorations and some of the costumes for Munich's annual press ball—a part of the famous *Fasching,* or carnival, which sets no limits to creative imagination or boisterous frolic.

Munich was the center of the arts in the Germany of those years. Just then the *Jugendstil,* as the Germans call *art nouveau* after the magazine *Die Jugend,* was giving way to a new movement in painting and the other arts—expressionism. In spontaneous, vivid outbursts, it depicted reality in a new way. Wassily Kandinsky, Paul Klee, Franz Marc, and Alexei von Jawlensky formed their famous *Blaue Reiter,* or Blue Rider, group in Munich at the time. Mendelsohn got to know them all, as well as numerous expressionist dancers, sculptors, musicians and writers who, with these painters, crowded the cafés to plot their revolution of modern art. These long, intense discussions probably had some impact on Mendelsohn's later work, although he always denied it. There is, at any rate, no doubt that he was also greatly influenced by the Belgian painter-architect Henry van de Velde.[15] And the enthusiasm of one of his friends, the *Jugendstil* architect Hermann Obrist, for oddly shaped bones, shells, and other organically shaped objects of nature, also made a deep impression on him.

More decisive for the shape Mendelsohn's architecture was to take was a trip to Holland he made some time later—shortly after the war. He was invited to lecture there when H. T. Wijdeveld, the editor of the architectural magazine *Wendingen,* which also helped to make the work of Frank Lloyd Wright known in Europe, published some of Mendelsohn's sketches. In Rotterdam he visited the famous housing development by J. J. P. Oud, a quintessence of coldly rational

De Stijl cubism. In Amsterdam and Hilversum he saw the work of H. P. Berlage, William Marinus Dudok, and Michael deKlerk—buildings of decidedly romantic and decorative intent. "Analytical Rotterdam refuses vision," Mendelsohn wrote to his wife. "Visionary Amsterdam does not understand cold objectivity. More than ever I stand by my reconciliatory program. Both are necessary, and both must find each other."[16]

Mendelsohn had opened his own office in Munich within days after he received his degree in architecture and engineering. Later he often regretted that he never worked in an architectural office to gain practical experience in technical matters, as the architectural registration laws now require, at least in the United States. He often had to rely on the ingenuity of his engineers in working out the structures he conceived.

As soon as Mendelsohn returned from the war he set up his office in Berlin. His first commission was the Einstein Tower, an observatory and laboratory which was to prove that the sun's spectral lines deviate from those of a terrestrial source of light, a part of the Theory of Relativity. The Mendelsohns had often discussed Albert Einstein's theory with a friend, the astro-physicist Erwin F. Freundlich, who worked with Einstein. It intrigued Mendelsohn, who made several sketches of observatories during the war; the sketches, in turn, intrigued Freundlich. The two helped to raise funds for this project from both public and private sources.

The telescope of the Einstein Tower, designed by Freundlich, is similar to that at Mount Wilson and projects the image of the sun or observed star to an underground laboratory—a thermo-constant room—where it can be spectographically analyzed and compared. The astronomical dome, with its six-foot-wide slit, can be turned to follow the rising and setting of all celestial bodies.

Mendelsohn conceived this structure in reinforced concrete. But during the construction, in the midst of Germany's drastic inflation, cement was suddenly rationed. Brick had to be substituted within the superstructure. This "fake" is often criticized, although no one seems to object because the walls of Le Corbusier's concrete chapel at Ronchamp are also of stone plastered with cement.[17] The Einstein Tower is still standing and in excellent repair (the photographs in this book were taken in 1959). When Mendelsohn was asked many years later if he would build it exactly that way again, he said, "God forbid! But whether I could build it again as well as I did in 1919, I don't know."[18] However that may be, the Einstein Tower has always remained the extreme, the irrational pole in Mendelsohn's work, and it had no visible influence on international architecture.

But it was an immediate sensation in Germany. The *Berliner Illustrierte,* a picture magazine then as popular in Germany as *Life* is in this country today, printed its picture on the cover. Just about that time—1921—the powerful publisher Lachmann-Mosse needed an addition to his *Berliner Tageblatt* building on one of Berlin's busiest downtown corners. He was interested in Mendelsohn. But could he risk giving this important assignment to an unknown Young Turk? He took what is now considered the more fashionable alternative to a personal decision and conducted a survey among his employees. Nearly all of them, it turned out, from his top editors down to the apprentices in the composing room, had seen the pictures of the Einstein Tower and were intrigued by it.

Mendelsohn got the job and had to enlarge his office. Among the assistants he employed was a young Austrian named Richard Neutra. The problem was to add three stories and a new corner façade to the nondescript, rather ornate old *Tageblatt* building, and Mendelsohn solved it by harmonizing the modern structure with the existing one (plate 11) instead of seeking a compromise with it. Hovering on the old building rather than weighing it down, the new stories sweep around the corner in an elegant flourish, visually supported by their own twelve-foot entrance canopy (plate 12).

A year later, Mendelsohn and Neutra entered a competition for a business center in Haifa, Palestine. The Egyptian pounds that the two received for winning this contest could, unlike the then worthless German mark, be exchanged for U. S. dollars. Neutra recalls with pleasure that this helped him to come to the United States and, as he put it, "to humanize a little the then current architectural cliches of that technologically leading country."[19] Whether he succeeded or not, it certainly did not take Richard Neutra long to rise to considerable and deserved fame. The Haifa business center, however, was never built. Neither were the buildings for a hydroelectric project, which had brought Mendelsohn to Palestine in the first place.

Mendelsohn's next trip, in 1924, took him to the United States, where he visited Frank Lloyd Wright at Taliesin, Wright's Wisconsin home. He was already much interested in Wright's work and, in his lectures and writings, was helping to make it known in Germany. His villa for Dr. Sternefeld on Berlin's Heerstrasse (plate 13), designed the previous year, seems far more Wrightian than Mendelsohnian. With its overlapping and interlocking brick and stucco squares, it strongly resembles the Robie House of 1909. Whether this resemblance is intentional or not, it is further evidence, if further evidence is needed, that Wright had a great influence in Europe long before he had any to speak of in his own country. When Mendelsohn, a year later, told the well-known Detroit architect Albert Kahn that he was about to visit Wright, Kahn said: "Who is this guy? Never heard of him."[20]

Mendelsohn and Wright, it seems, agreed on the relationship between music and architecture but disagreed on American materialism. Mendelsohn defended his beloved Bach against Wright's partiality for Beethoven, and Wright defended his country against Mendelsohn's criticism. Since Mendelsohn spoke little English at the time, Neutra, who was working with Wright, did the interpreting. He recalls that he considerably toned down both Mendelsohn's somewhat disparaging remarks and Wright's rather haughty retorts to the young German blade. "I am proud that my translating job cemented a life-long sympathy between the two," he has said. "That's what instantaneous translation should accomplish—besides a splitting headache to the interpreter."

The second morning of Mendelsohn's visit, a pleasant Sunday, was devoted to a walk along the Wisconsin River. According to the Swiss architect Werner M. Moser, who was also present, the smooth river bank tempted Wright to draw in the sand and he playfully suggested a contest. Mendelsohn, Moser remembers, drew one of his round, flowing fantasies, while Wright sketched an angular building, typical of his style at that time. Mercifully, there seems to have been no judgment to wreck Neutra's diplomacy.

Moser met Wright in Paris thirteen years later, in 1937. He wrote to Mrs. Mendelsohn after her husband's death that on that occasion Wright showed him his latest designs and that he "was fascinated to see Wright's first rounded forms in the plan and elevation of his concept for the Johnson Wax building. Actually, they were rounded corners which in his later designs developed into circular shapes or partial circles. Yet, at that time in Paris, I was struck by a certain analogy to Mendelsohn's work. It was merely a personal impression and we didn't talk about it at all. History shows clearly and often that personalities can inspire each other without either the possibility or the need for mathematical proof of such influence."[21]

"All art is performance."

—ROBERT FROST

3. SUCCESS WITHOUT COMPROMISE

ON HIS RETURN to Berlin, Mendelsohn was asked to design a factory for the Leningrad Textile Trust (plate 14). His much-publicized ventilation system for the Luckenwalde hat factory dyeing plant—a kind of horizontal chimney—had attracted the attention of the Russians, who asked him to repeat this efficient innovation. In Leningrad he raised the drying lofts to soaring, slightly tapered shafts atop three low, parallel halls and made them a dominant feature. Despite its many diverse units, the model for this large industrial complex—the total length of the building is about one mile—shows an amazingly unified composition of considerable interest and beauty. Seven years later, for an even larger plant— a zinc factory in Magdeburg (plate 37)—he again turned functional elements, in this case huge chimneys, into an ingenious aesthetic asset.

His work in Leningrad brought Mendelsohn into contact with Soviet life and, as he had done upon his return from the States, he wrote a somewhat aphoristic book about it. He seems to have had a hard time with most Russian architects who, he complained, were obsessed with palatial formalism and had a penchant for wasting valuable space with forests of columns. This Soviet addiction to wedding-cake architecture, which is only now beginning to fade, became evident to the entire world a few years later.

In 1928 the Kremlin, *mirabile dictu,* allowed an international competition for

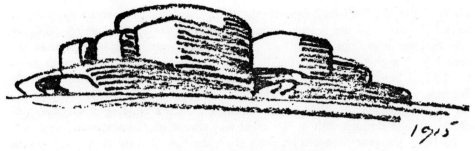

Sketch for Grain Elevator, 1915

the Palace of the Soviets in Moscow. Mendelsohn, along with Le Corbusier, Perret, Poelzig, Gropius, and a very few others were commissioned to submit designs, and there were some 450 voluntary entries. The program called for two assembly halls for 15,000 and 6,000 people respectively, in addition to a library, smaller halls, exhibition space, and administrative offices. Mendelsohn's solution (plate 35) was among the few which combined the two large halls into one unit.[22] He divided two facing domes of different sizes with a tall rectangular block comprising the other needed spaces. The model is again reminiscent of his early sketches and could also easily be one of the most recent structures of the as-yet-unnamed new shell-vault architecture of today. It was obviously much too radical for the Soviets. They rejected all the entries and instead chose to build one of the worst architectural atrocities of the century.

Mendelsohn's most brilliant and perhaps, at the time, most imitated buildings are his four famous department stores built from 1926 to 1929 for Schocken in Nuremberg, Stuttgart (plates 16–18), and Chemnitz (plates 19, 20), and for Petersdorff in Breslau (plates 21, 22). Up to that time department stores were generally clumsy imitations of massive Renaissance palaces, with oversized windows on the ground floor for display. Mendelsohn was the first modern architect who had the opportunity to make this contemporary institution look contemporary. He made it efficient and dramatic to boot. His stores are architectural showmanship at its best—not in the sense of being Disneyland stunts, but because of their interesting and dynamic structures, their exquisite taste, and their tender attention to luxurious detail. It is true, as Jürgen Joedicke points out, that Mendelsohn raised the horizontality of his window ribbons almost to the level of a dogma. But, in the days before luminous ceilings and air conditioning, these glass ribbons served a decidedly functional purpose. They provide light for the sales counters placed beneath them, and for the entire store interior as well, without offending the retina. And lit up from within at night, they make for a fascinating display which commands attention without being as offensive as advertising on that scale would be.

The most attractive of these buildings, and perhaps the most significant architecturally, was the Stuttgart Schocken store. Its long lines of windows, interlaid with brick and travertine, are abruptly arrested by a cantilevered staircase tower

21

which breaks the horizontal movement. "With the dramatic contrast between the formal elements and the sharply defined features of the façade," writes Joedicke, "the building offers one of the best solutions to department-store design of this period."[23] Yet this handsome building was demolished in 1960 to make room for a larger enterprise. Protests from just about every prominent architect in the Western world were of no avail. "Mendelsohn would have been the last to care," his widow consoled herself as much as others. "Once a building of his was completed, he was through with it. His mind was always on the next one."

In 1928, the year Mendelsohn worked on the last of these department stores, the Schocken *Warenhaus* at Chemnitz, he also designed his famous headquarters for the Metal Workers' Union in Berlin (plates 23–26), which later, ironically, was to become the national headquarters of the Nazi Labor Front. This building makes the most of a triangular lot. At the corner a convex façade is gripped by lower wings which sweep back at a dramatic angle. The emphasis is again strongly horizontal, accented by an interesting turret on the corner façade which holds a flagpole and gives the building a ship-like forward movement.

Like his department stores, Mendelsohn's movie palace, the Universum on Berlin's Kurfürstendamm (plates 27, 28), was among the first modern designs for its purpose. The sweeping curves of this building, one piled on top of another in receding layers, pierced by a narrow rectangular tower, are again dramatic and original. The auditorium, which seated 1,800 (it has now been divided into two theaters), was especially admired at the time for its sweep and novelty (plate 28).

The Universum was a part of a large city development plan which was also to include a cabaret, a hotel, and stores around a shopping plaza, with apartment houses (plate 29) in the rear. The scope of this scheme was eventually considerably reduced. But Mendelsohn's design, like that for the rebuilding of Berlin's two most important squares, Alexanderplatz and Potsdamerplatz, is especially interesting. His great talent for spatial rhythm, continuity, and dramatic interplay of forms is here applied to a city-planning scheme, which has lost none of its validity in the intervening years. For Alexanderplatz (plate 30), Mendelsohn envisioned a raised, semicircular building which would bridge two wide radiating streets and thus encircle the space. On Potsdamerplatz (plate 31) he would have created a second, octagonal plaza, opening into the existing square at the point where two charming historic buildings—little Greek temples designed by Karl Friedrich Schinkel early in the nineteenth century—faced each other across Leipzigerstrasse. Neither design was carried out.

His Columbus House (plates 32–34) was to be the first building of Mendelsohn's Potsdamerplatz scheme. The fate of this "little skyscraper," as it has been called, which was perhaps the most attractive modern building in downtown Berlin, illustrates the grim drama of that city's recent history. It was started in 1931 and completed in one year. By the end of another year, it housed dreaded Gestapo torture chambers. Badly damaged in the bombing raids, it was rebuilt by the East German Communists, who turned it into one of their state-owned stores, presumably to impress people in the Western Sector across Potsdamerplatz. That is, possibly, also why the workers who rebelled against the East

German Communist regime on June 17, 1953, set fire to the Columbus House. To erase this memory the Communists have now also erased the building.

But nobody even dreamed these nightmares when, in 1930, Mendelsohn built his own house "Am Rupenhorn" on a quiet suburban street along Havelsee, one of Berlin's many lovely lakes (plates 38–42). It was his great extravagance, an orgy of perfectionism. Yet the design of the building is most restrained and quietly elegant. Along the entire garden front is a generous terrace. The glass walls of the large main-floor rooms disappear into the basement at the push of a button. Almost everything, including even telephones and musical instruments, has a specially and beautifully designed cabinet or is built in. No standard equipment is used anywhere; even the silver and linen were specially designed and made for this dream house.

The Mendelsohns entertained many of Europe's cultural elite in this home and several now-prominent American architects came to visit. Mendelsohn was then at the height of his fame and achievements. He was the first *successful* modern architect, pleasing his clients and all but the most reactionary critics and winning numerous competitions. He received commissions for important buildings such as none of the other masters of his generation ever got the opportunity to execute. Yet he never compromised his artistic intent. To a client who asked him to repeat a previous design he replied: "Would you have asked Beethoven for the Seventh Symphony when he was ready to create the Ninth? All I'll say is, you'll get a Mendelsohn!" And a Mendelsohn always remained as militantly modern as any building of the avant-garde—with one difference, perhaps. Mendelsohn's architecture is always considerate of the surroundings, it fits gracefully and politely into the land- or city-scape. This is particularly evident in his work in Palestine, but it is true of his earlier and later periods as well. There is, for instance, much of the verve and flamboyance of a Mendelsohn sketch in Frank Lloyd Wright's Guggenheim Museum. But Mendelsohn would never have dumped such an inappropriate structure so arrogantly onto New York's Fifth Avenue.

The Mendelsohns enjoyed their fabulous house on Havel Lake only a little more than two years. Then Hitler confronted them, as he did most creative Germans, with the bitter alternative of death or exile.

"Art is a harmony parallel to that of nature."

—PAUL CÉZANNE

4. BUILDING IN THE SUN

MENDELSOHN LEFT GERMANY in March 1933 at the age of forty-five. He was tired of practicing architecture, or just tired. Briefly an earlier idea lured him: a

European Academy of Art on the shores of the Mediterranean. He had often discussed it with his friends the Dutch architect Wijdeveld and the French painter Amédée Ozenfant, and he now pursued it from Holland. The three had a prospectus printed, raised some money, and bought a beautiful site near St. Raphael on the French Riviera. He and Wijdeveld were to teach architecture. Ozenfant, the composer Paul Hindemith, and the English sculptor-typographer Eric Gill were to be among the faculty. But soon difficulties developed. Besides, on a trip to England, Mendelsohn was most cordially welcomed and urged to stay. This unexpected enthusiasm for his work quickly rekindled his own. He opened his office in London in partnership with a promising young architect, Serge Chermayeff.

As one of their first projects the two partners entered the competition for a summer resort recreation center in Bexhill, on the Sussex coast. They won over about two hundred competitors. The De La Warr Pavilion (plates 43–46) is not daringly original, but it undoubtedly helped to advance modern architecture in England. Its generous terraces and balconies spell vacation and relaxation and the semicircular staircase tower, ringed with balconies, gives the building a gay, lyrical quality.

Mendelsohn did a number of other buildings in England, but even before the Bexhill Pavilion was dedicated, he had shifted his more important activities to Palestine. This time he was invited by Chaim Weizmann, who wanted Mendelsohn to design a residence for him at Rehoboth, near Tel Aviv. Mendelsohn had known the eminent Zionist statesman-scientist, who was to become the first president of Israel, for some time and had supported the Zionist movement since his student days. When Weizmann's commission was followed by others in Palestine, he commuted from England by plane for a while. Soon, however, he settled in Jerusalem, fascinated by the challenge of a new contribution to a new society.

In his dozen or so Palestine buildings of all types, Mendelsohn changed his entire style and subordinated his mastery of singing lines and glazed circles to the needs of an entirely different environment. His exuberance turns to the interiors; the exteriors politely adjust themselves to their surroundings. These buildings answer the often-raised question whether modern architecture may honestly express regional and national differences. Mies, for one, holds that the airplane and our other new conveniences, not to speak of building technology, are now the same everywhere in the world, and that, therefore, only the obvious variations in climate justify any special distinction between a building on the shores of Lake Michigan and one serving the same purpose on the shores of the Mediterranean.[24] But Mendelsohn's architecture in Haifa and Jerusalem is different from his previous work not only because he had to shelter his clients from a hot and glaring sun, or even because he had to use different materials, mostly stone. They are decidedly distinct because he also deeply felt the impact of Palestine's strange and beautiful landscape and its ancient and diverse culture.

The Weizmann residence (plates 47–51) is situated on a hill, in the midst of an orange plantation, and commands a magnificent view. As with all Mendelsohn's Palestinian buildings, its orientation takes careful advantage of prevailing breezes.

The house is deliberately stately, designed for large receptions and prestige. On the outside, however, only a circular staircase tower, striped vertically with sun screens, announces its importance. Otherwise the plain, angular building detaches itself from its hot and unpredictable surroundings and opens itself only to its interior cooling center—a patio with a swimming pool. As always, Mendelsohn lavished special attention on the garden. He read up on Palestine's flora and exasperated experienced gardeners when he insisted on transplanting century-old olive trees. To their amazement, the trees are still flourishing.

The Weizmann residence and the Government Hospital at Haifa (plates 66–69) are built for the plains and therefore their reinforced concrete structure is faced with a white stucco finish, in keeping with Levantine tradition. Mendelsohn's Jerusalem buildings—a residence and a library for his old client Salman Schocken (plates 52, 53), the Anglo-Palestine Bank (plates 63–65), and the Hadassah University Medical Center on Mount Scopus (plates 54–62)—are of stone. This is a local requirement to assure that new buildings in the Holy City harmonize with its ancient or merely aged architecture. Mendelsohn's stone buildings certainly look built of stone. They are square-cut and serene. Their elegance relies on proportion and their sparse embellishments on the shadows cast by the varying patterns and shapes of the deeply set window openings. Only here or there is there an almost reluctant flamboyant touch, such as the little roofed balcony of the Schocken house, or the decorative double flagpole on the Anglo-Palestine Bank, which is fastened on the front of the building not much above the ground to relieve a blank section of the façade (plate 63). It recalls the flagpole turret on the Metal Workers' building in Berlin almost ten years earlier (plate 23). The Hadassah hospital on Mount Scopus (plates 54–62), with its marvelous view over the ancient walled city to one side and the Judean desert and the Moab mountains to the other (plate 54), holds a special surprise: a turret-like little chapel which juts out over the mountainside, open to the grandeur of the panorama and the limitless sky beyond (plates 61, 62).

The Agricultural College at Rehoboth (plates 70–72) shows how well Mendelsohn was able to express the purpose of a building along with native architectural tradition. It could hardly be anything but a training ground for dedicated youngsters determined to explore all modern means to make an ancient and arid soil productive. The pitched roof, covered with red-brown tile, helps, of course, to give the building a rustic character, but it does so without being in the least sentimental.

Despite the constant unrest of the times—most people carried arms even during the day—Mendelsohn was again happy and intensely absorbed in the challenge of his work. He lived and had his office in a romantic old windmill just where the new Jerusalem begins. He had many friends among both British and Jewish leaders and ardently discussed with them the birth pangs of the Jewish state. He wanted the new Israel to build well-planned, proud, beautiful cities and structures and hoped to be appointed chief government architect and planner to help to realize this ambition. Nothing came of this, in part because the outbreak of war stopped nearly all building activity. He tried to join the British Army but was refused because of his age (he was fifty-three by now) and the fact that he was not a native-born British citizen. Nor was he encouraged to return to London. The Blitz had started and noncombatants were only in the way. Palestine offered little hope for an income sufficient to help the many family members who had been dependent on him since fleeing the Nazis.

In March 1941 he left for the United States and another new beginning.

"But when the day of anguish has arrived,
And nothing stops the course of time,
Accept, America, the hearts that free survived,
Make Europe's last free heroes thine!"

—AUGUST GRAF VON PLATEN (1818)

5. *THE SYNAGOGUES*

IF MENDELSOHN'S BUILDINGS in Palestine seem to depart from his "first idea"— his exuberant plasticity—it is because he wisely yielded to the power of the area's culture. In the United States there is no such pervading, general environment. Each building is, or is considered to be, a new challenge. We have not as yet settled on national, regional, or even city-wide criteria for architectural expression, and perhaps we never will. We frown upon considerations of aesthetic harmony as an un-American regimentation of our passion for self-expression and originality. Since air conditioning was developed, even the differences in climate across our country have less and less effect on our living habits and thus on the functional demands we make on our buildings.

This absence of restraints permitted Mendelsohn once more to return with full creative élan to the kind of architecture his early sketches visualized. Particularly the seven synagogues and community centers he designed here, of which unfortunately only four have actually been built, are highly original, personal statements. New forms again flow into or arrest each other in dramatic variety and yet the whole is cast from the same mold. There is always some visual surprise, a delightful one, from every new vantage point, proving, as Mendelsohn once put it, that "good architecture is designed around the corner." Some people consider this architecture too emotional. Many others, however, find that his synagogues fulfill the function Nikolaus Pevsner said a religious building ought to have: to "convert visitors into worshippers."[25]

The war years gave Mendelsohn the opportunity, however involuntary, to reflect and to get oriented in the United States. For a while he served as a consultant to

Sketch for World University, Berkeley Hills, California, 1943

the War Department. But the better part of this time he lived, largely on a Guggenheim Fellowship, in Croton-on-Hudson in the house of a family friend. From there he traveled a good deal and lectured at a number of architectural schools. He had a special knack for provoking and challenging his students and was extremely popular with most. His reputation among architects had, of course, preceded him to this country and was further boosted by a retrospective exhibition of his work which opened at the New York Museum of Modern Art on the day of Pearl Harbor.

Nevertheless, Mendelsohn's uncompromising and unconventional ways of dealing with clients and colleagues often resulted in friction and irritation. He felt at times that he was not properly understood in this country, and that architects are not as much respected here as in Europe. But he was constantly stimulated anew by the promise of American civilization and considered himself a part of America's future. He loved this country and its landscape. In the diary-sketchbook he kept on his travels he compared Mount Vernon with Mont-Saint-Michel, called California's redwood trees "God's own flagpoles," and enthusiastically fantasized about a huge bridge across Grand Canyon, which to him represented nature's "blue period."

San Francisco inspired his poetic bent to one of its most lyrical summits: "Take the serene circle of Athen's violet bay—its focus the Acropolis," he told a lecture audience, "or the shimmering parabola of the blue bay of Naples—the Vesuvius its fateful axis; the narrow straits of towering Corinth, or the wide extent of desert surrounding Alexandria; the glamorous ports of the Orient—Basra and Bombay— or the silent granite gorges of Corsica's harbors; take the poetic azure of France's south coast, or the dramatic splendor of Istanbul and its Golden Horn—count their special values as high as you wish—and San Francisco will still exceed their sum total; mix their best colors to one exciting hue—and San Francisco will still outshine it."[26] Needless to say, he settled there.

San Francisco did not return Mendelsohn's compliments with equal generosity when he opened his office there in 1945, at first in a short-lived partnership with John E. Dinwiddie and Albert Hill. Aside from a prosaic laboratory for the Atomic Energy Commission at Berkeley and an electronics laboratory, these com-

Sketch for Russell House, San Francisco, California, 1948

missions coming a good while after he had settled in San Francisco, he was given only two opportunities to contribute to Bay Area architecture: the Maimonides Hospital in 1946 and a residence for Mr. and Mrs. Leon B. Russell in 1950.

The Maimonides Hospital (plates 73, 74) was originally designed and built as a home for the chronically sick. Mendelsohn developed the plan in depth on an impossibly small, 100-foot-wide lot. He placed the eleven-story hospital proper in the center, shielded from the noisy slum streets on either side by auxiliary buildings. Its main feature is the lovely balconies which swing out in rhythmic curves and which, with their delicate white balustrades, give the effect of lacy ribbons. Their uncannily lithe effect is due in part to the fact that they taper out to an incredibly slim two inches. Van de Velde called this building "a great and noble gesture toward the last step, that of pure beauty."[27]

Unfortunately, however, that beauty did not last. Soon after the completion of the building it changed hands and the new owners converted it into an old-age home, an enterprise which proved unprofitable. Mendelsohn's original scheme could have increased the number of beds from 83 to 143. It called for two additional stories, topped by a covered roof garden. But he was not consulted. Instead, another architect filled in the balconies to gain additional space. Besides ruining the appearance of the building, this, as Mendelsohn predicted, also increased the air conditioning cost, for his balconies had the functional purpose of shading the windows below.

The Russell House (plates 75–77) is an L-shaped redwood building whose main wing is raised above the ground on slim steel columns to make the very best of the gorgeous view. The space below adds to the patio of the smallish lot and connects it with the terrace in front, besides framing a panorama of the Golden Gate. In addition to another joyous, if somewhat compressed, Mendelsohn stair-

28

case, this house has a courageously cantilevered circular turret at the corner, echoed by semicircular adaptations of the San Francisco bay window.

Mendelsohn's first synagogue was also his first actual commission in the United States—the temple and community center for the Congregation B'nai Amoona in St. Louis (plates 80–84). At that time, the end of 1945, most congregations in the United States still took a dim view of contemporary architecture. Christians, in architect Harold Spitznagel's words, believed that "the only gateway to Heaven is a Gothic arch," Jews pusillanimously clung to what little tradition there is in American synagogue architecture—mostly adaptations of Romanesque or Byzantine domes concocted into a mishmash which has been aptly described as "meshugothic." There were, of course, some notable exceptions. But still, it was "an act of optimism," as Le Corbusier called the thirteenth-century cathedrals, to attempt an honest and thus contemporary religious building. Mendelsohn courageously committed the act.

His basic plan takes account of the fact that two and three times as many people flock to services on the High Holidays as on a normal Sabbath. To accommodate this overflow he adjoined the sanctuary, the entrance foyer, and the social hall, dividing them with disappearing walls and folding doors. When these partitions are removed and temporary seats are put up, the sanctuary is expanded from its normal 600 seats to 1,500. The expansion can, of course, also be limited to the foyer alone, as the plan shows (plate 81).

This solution, which Mendelsohn used in various ways for all his synagogues and which by now has become almost standard, was not entirely original with him. But he applied it unusually well by harmonizing his foyers and assembly rooms in scale, color, and interior decoration with the prayer hall. This is particularly true of his Temple Emanu-El at Grand Rapids, Michigan (plates 92–94). There is no makeshift at all when this sanctuary is enlarged. It is parallel to the social hall and the two constitute one large room which is divided down the middle by a power-operated folding wall. A tapestry-like mural by Lucienne Bloch Dimitroff, which covers the rear wall, is similarly split. When the two rooms combined are used for services, the ark moves into the center. The track of the folding wall is contained in a fin-like strip atop the roof of the butterfly-shaped building.

Mendelsohn's community centers are just that—centers. Whether the site is small, as in St. Louis, or spacious, as in Cleveland (plates 85–88), the synagogue, school, social and administrative units combine into an integrated design. They are not unlike medieval monasteries, in that religious and mundane buildings unite for a total religious purpose and shelter each other from the noise and confusion of the outside world. And as in most monasteries (and in contrast to many present-day suburban religious centers, where the church or synagogue seems quite incidental), Mendelsohn's temples declare themselves proudly and boldly. The St. Louis temple is under a sweeping parabola which projects far beyond the front windows and shields them from the western exposure. The Mount Zion Temple in St. Paul, originally conceived in 1950 as a series of towering triangular arches (plates 89–91)—not unlike Skidmore, Owings & Merrill's design for the

29

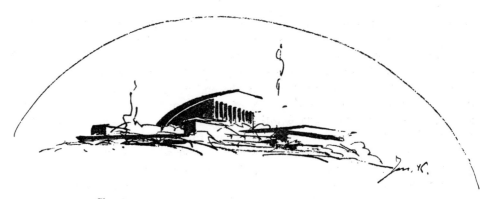

Sketch for Temple B'nai Amoona, St. Louis, Missouri, 1946

Air Force Academy chapel of 1953—is a serene, copper-clad slab (now oxidizing to a lovely hue) with strongly emphasized outside frames, towering above a cubic composition of low buildings.

All these forms make impressive interiors. But whether dome, parabola, or soaring shaft, the structure itself is even more effective inside. It evokes a thrill. And it creates an atmosphere which, blended with the glory of sunlight—there are no mysteries in the Jewish service of this country—and the play of contrasts, color, texture, and Mendelsohn's always polished but never slick use of rich materials, seldom fails to evoke an emotional response.

The three synagogue designs which were never built again show entirely different forms. The model for the Temple Emanu-El at Dallas (plate 99) calls for a lofty, conical structure backed by a fan-shaped social hall and towering above a flowing arrangement of other buildings on a large, wooded site. The interior space of this tall cone, lighted by narrow clerestory windows, is fascinating to contemplate. For the temple of the Washington (D. C.) Hebrew Congregation he designed a tall slab on top of a hill overlooking a lake (plate 100). For the Congregation Beth El in Baltimore, which built a school wing of his design, Mendelsohn proposed a temple topped by a triple barrel vault, the overhang of which is cut back at an angle (plates 95, 96). Mendelsohn designed this building in 1948. But the sketches (plates 97, 98) might well have been among those exhibited at Cassirer's gallery in Berlin thirty years earlier. Yet the structure has lost none of its freshness; in fact, barrel vaults are just now coming into vogue.

Not long before his death, of cancer, on September 15, 1953, Mendelsohn made two designs for a proposed memorial to the six million Jews murdered by the Nazis. The City of New York dedicated a piece of Riverside Park, along the Hudson, for the purpose, in return for the right to veto the design. The first veto was of Percival Goodman's proposal, for which Jacques Lipchitz was to be the sculptor. Mendelsohn submitted a design for an assembly hall with a scultpure by Mitzi Salomon, for he believed, as did many others, that the monument ought

30

to serve a living purpose (plate 102). A tall, open structure, which symbolizes the stone tablets of the Ten Commandments, is in the rear of the hall as if to declare its hallowed character. This, too, was vetoed. The second version (plate 103) is reduced to a more or less conventional monument of the kind which today somehow fails to inspire. The eighty-foot tables are now solid stone and situated on a rather forbidding stone platform cut into the side of a hill. For this design Ivan Mestrovic was to sculpture a wall relief. But for various reasons the entire idea fell by the wayside.

While working on one of his last projects—a synagogue—Mendelsohn wrote to his wife: "Not much sleep . . . too excited at the prospect of doing something extraordinary, eternal. A new religious structure for a new religious meaning."[28]

"Extraordinary" seems too trite a word to apply to these fresh concepts. "Eternal"? It takes a while to assess the validity of this aspiration. But it does seem already apparent that there now exists in the United States, probably for the first time anywhere, a distinct style of synagogue architecture, a new religious structure. In 1946, when Mendelsohn designed the St. Louis temple, this was at best a hope. Many other outstanding architects, among them Percival Goodman, Max Abramovitz, Karl Kamrath, and Richard M. Bennett, have contributed to this development. Mendelsohn's speeches, writing, projects, and actual buildings have, however, as Bennett says, given it an initial verve, enthusiasm and impetus.[29]

Nor is Mendelsohn's influence confined to modern synagogues. Like all revolutions, the architectural revolution of Mendelsohn's time threatened to turn rebellion into a new dogma. In rebellion against futile and eclectic efforts to revive the past, it rigidly pronounced that all architecture of the future must be reduced to its barest and squarest essentials. Mendelsohn's art was never constricted by such dogma. He "stood for freedom, imagination, and creative individual leadership," as the dean of the University of California school of architecture, William W. Wuster, said at Mendelsohn's funeral. Since then, from Idlewild to Sidney, a new architecture in steel and reinforced concrete is rising in the shape of Mendelsohn's visual prophecies. The freedom, imagination and creative individual leadership Mendelsohn demonstrated in his buildings are beginning to replace monotonous cubic austerity. Beauty, or at least the artistic intent to create it, is again counted among the functions of a building.

Is Mendelsohn, as van de Velde has written, making a "definite imprint on the style of the twentieth century"?[30] Any answer to this question is conjecture. Even if we could measure the exact dimensions of the imprint an artist makes on his time, would it really matter? Mendelsohn's intent was never to create a style. He only wanted to create beautiful buildings.

The Notes to the Text begin on page 113.

The drawings by Eric Mendelsohn reproduced on the following pages are reduced to three-fifths of their original size, with the exception of drawing 46 which is reduced to two-fifths of its original size.

1. Imaginary sketch, 1914; pencil
2. Airport, 1914; ink
3. Market Hall, 1914; ink

4. Imaginary sketch, 1914; India ink

5. Observatories, 1917; pencil

6. Railway station, 1914; ink

7. Warehouse, 1914; ink

8. Imaginary sketch, 1914; ink

9. Gas factory, 1914; ink

10. Imaginary sketch, 1914; ink
11. Factory with crane, 1914; pencil
12. Railway station, 1914; ink

13. Optical Factory, 1917; ink
14, 15. Railway station, 1914-15; India ink

16

16. Residence, 1915; pencil

17

17. Dedication to the birth of
Esther Mendelsohn, 1916; ink

18

18. Garden Pavilion, Luckenwalde,
1920; India ink

19

20

21

22

23

24

19. Industrial building with crane, 1917; pencil
20. Cantilevered skyscraper, 1919; ink
21. Imaginary sketch, 1917; pencil

22. Industrial building, 1914; ink
23. Imaginary sketch, 1917
24. Film studio, 1914; India ink

25

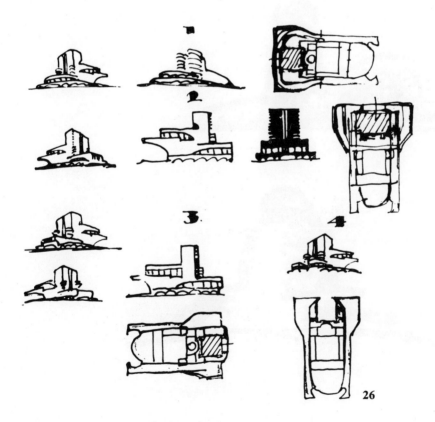

26

25. Imaginary sketch, 1917
26. Optical factory study sheet, 1917; ink, pencil and crayon

27

28

29

27-29. Einstein Tower, Potsdam, 1920
(top sketch: pencil, center: crayon)

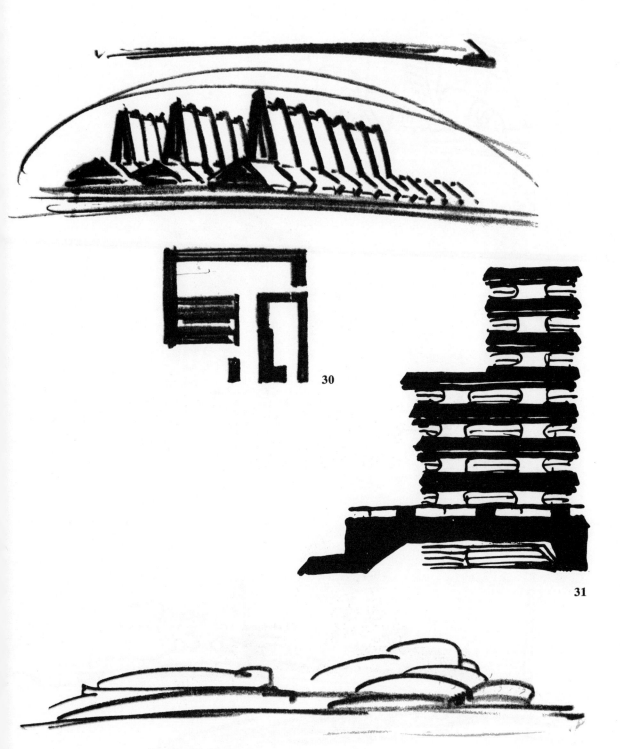

30. Textile Dye Plant, Leningrad, 1926; pencil

31. Skyscraper, Kemperplatz, Berlin, 1921; India ink

32. Universum Theatre and Cinema, Berlin, 1925-28; red pencil

33. Imaginary sketch, 1920-30; ink

34. Bridgehead, 1920; ink

35. Garden Pavilion, Luckenwalde, 1920; India ink

36. Garden Pavilion, Luckenwalde, 1920; ink

37. Imaginary sketch, 1921-30; pencil

38. Mosse Pavilion, Press Exhibition, Cologne, 1928; pencil

39

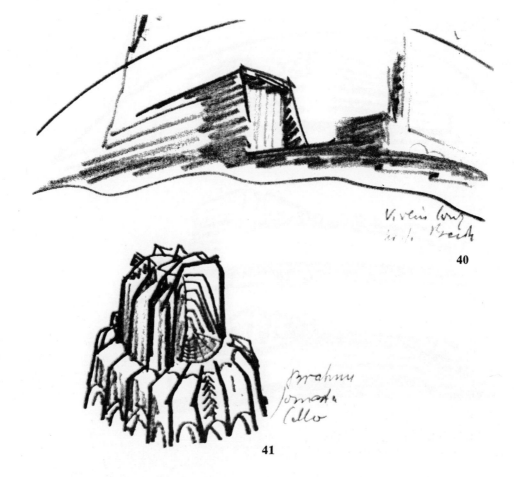

40

41

39. "Toccata in D Major," 1921-30; pencil
40. "Violin Concerto," Bach, 1921-29; pencil
41. "Cello Sonata," Brahms, 1921-29; pencil

42

42. Schocken Department Store, Stuttgart, 1926-28; pencil

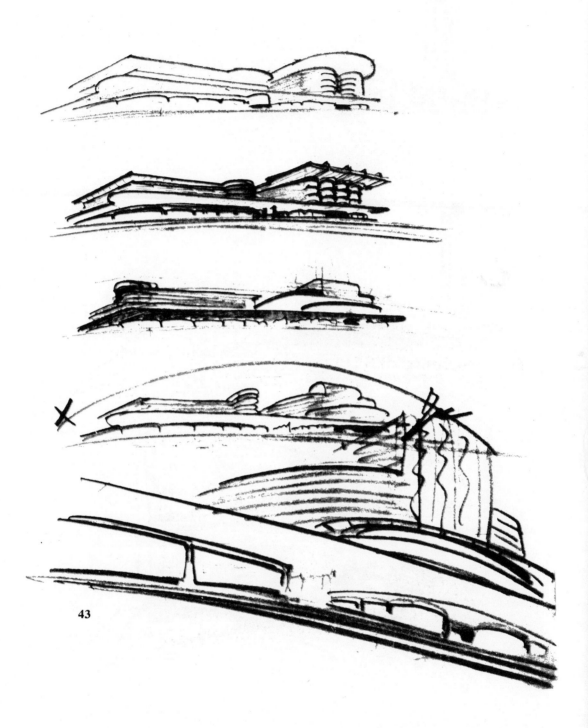

43

43. Universum Theatre and Cinema, Berlin, 1925-28; red and black pencil

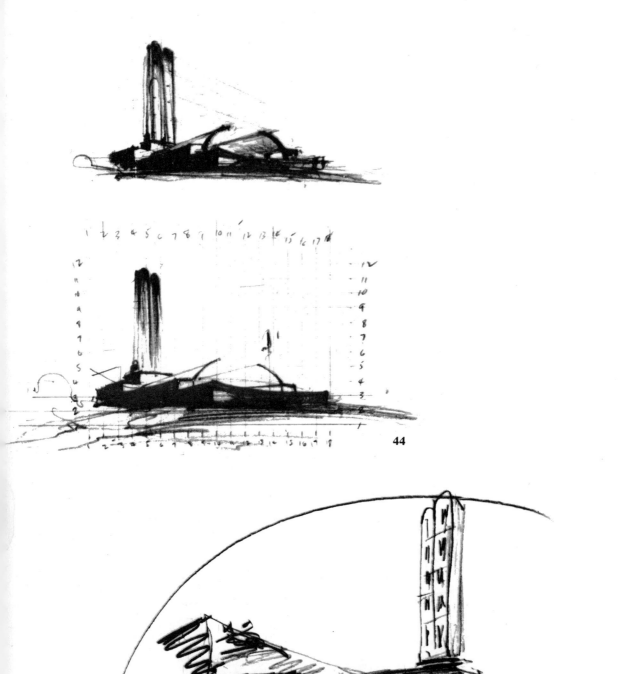

44, 45. Monuments to six million Jews killed by the Nazis, 1949; pencil
(top sketch: first design, bottom: second design)

4. Einstein Tower, Potsdam, 1919.

2. Le Corbusier. Chapel at Ronchamp, France, 1955. Detail, waterspout.

4. Einstein Tower. Detail, waterspout.

3. Antonio Gaudí. Casa Milá, Barcelona, 1905-10. Detail.

5. Einstein Tower. Exterior detail.

Einstein Tower. Exterior detail.

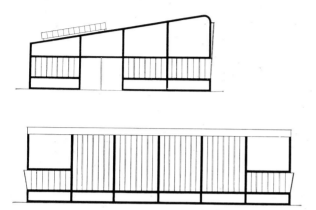

7. Hat Factory, Luckenwalde. Elevations.

8. Hat Factory, Luckenwalde, Interior.

9. Hat Factory, Luckenwalde, 1920.

10. Hat Factory, Luckenwalde. Exterior.

. Berliner Tageblatt Building Addition, 1921-22.

. Berliner Tageblatt Building Addition. Entrance
nopy.

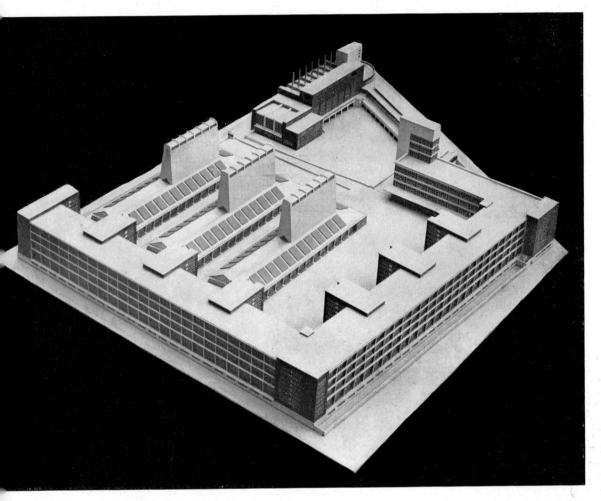

14. Textile Factory, Leningrad Textile Trust, 1925. Model.

Villa Sternefeld, Heerstrasse, Berlin, 1923 (opposite page).

15. Herpich Store, Berlin, 1924. Interior.

16. Schocken Department Store, Stuttgart, 1926-27.

Schocken Store, Stuttgart. Corner pavilion (opposite page).

18. Schocken Store, Stuttgart. Staircase.

19. Schocken Department Store, Chemnitz, 1928-29.

20. Schocken Store, Chemnitz.

22. Petersdorff Store. Night view.

...ersdorff Department Store, Breslau, 1926-27 (opposite page).

23. Metal Worker's Union Building, Berlin, 1929.

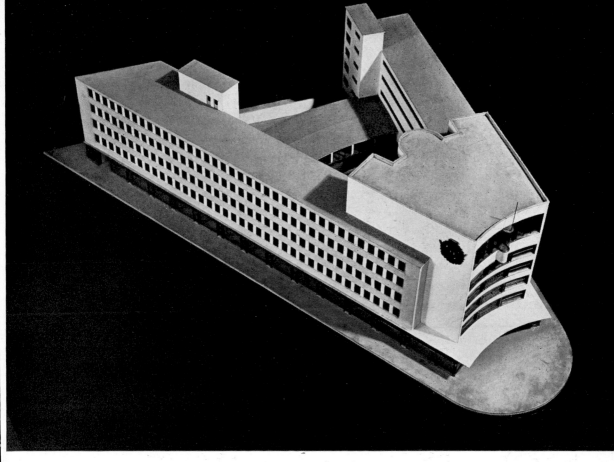

24. Metal Worker's Union. Model.

25. Metal Worker's Union. Rear view of model.

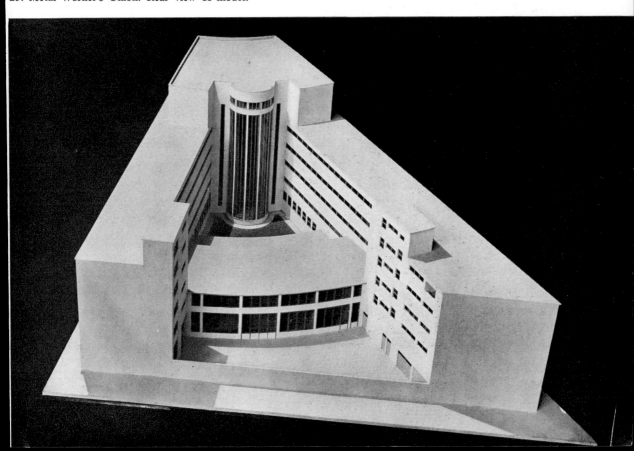

26. Metal Worker's Union. Staircase.

27. Universum Motion Picture
Theatre, Kurfürstendamm,
Berlin, 1927-28.

28. Universum Theatre. Interior.

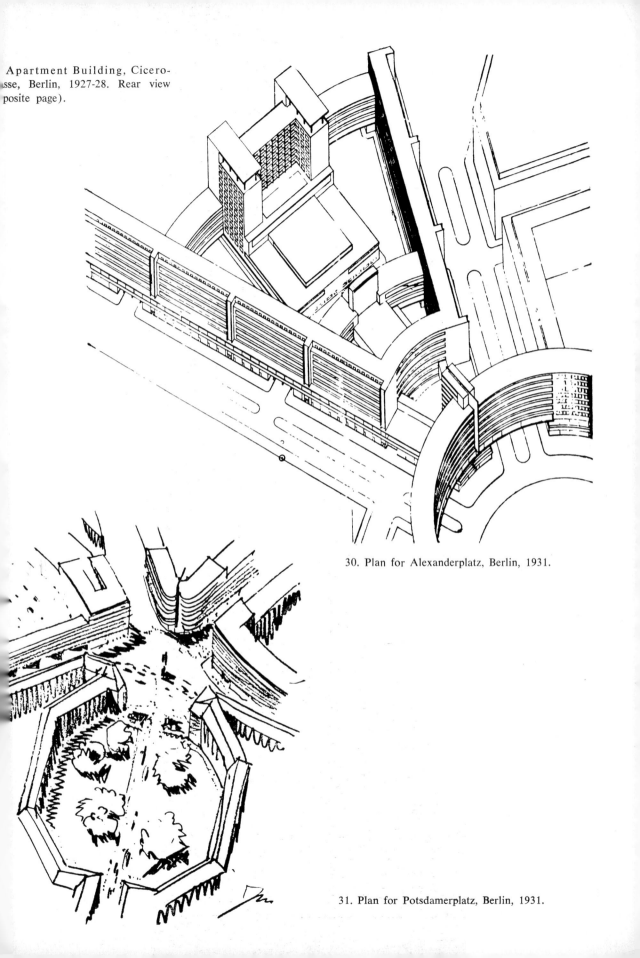

Apartment Building, Cicero-
sse, Berlin, 1927-28. Rear view
posite page).

30. Plan for Alexanderplatz, Berlin, 1931.

31. Plan for Potsdamerplatz, Berlin, 1931.

32. Columbus House.

33. Columbus House.

34. Columbus House, Potsdamerplatz, Berli
Rear view.

35. Palace of the Soviets Competition, 1929. Model. (*not executed*)

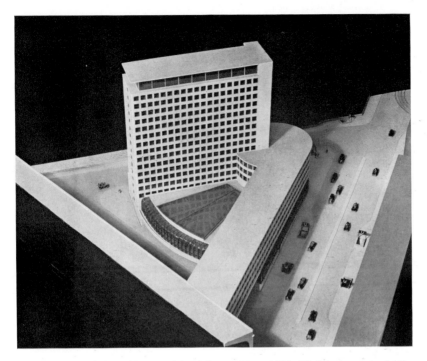

36. Berlin Transit Company Building Competition, 1931. Model. (*not executed*)

37. Zinc Factory, Magdeburg. 1931. Model.

38. Mendelsohn's own house, "Am Rupenhorn," Berlin, 1929-30.

39. "Am Rupenhorn." Exterior.

40. "Am Rupenhorn." Interior detail.

41. "Am Rupenhorn." Livingroom.

42. "Am Rupenhorn." Bedroom.

43. De La Warr Pavilion, Bexhill, land, 1933-34. Staircase (opposite p

44. De La Warr Pavilion. Balcony, staircase tower.

45. De La Warr Pavilion. Exterior.

46. De La Warr Pavilion. Staircase tower.

47. Chaim Weizmann House, Rehoboth, Israel, 1935-36.

48. Weizmann House. Exterior.

49. Weizmann House. Staircase.

50. Weizmann House. Interior court with pool.

51. Weizmann House. Staircase.

52. Salman Schocken House, Jerusalem, 1936.

54. Hadassah University Medical Center, M
Scopus, Jerusalem, 1936-38 (opposite pa

55. Hadassah Medical Center. Detail, main entrance.

56. Hadassah Medical Center. Main entrance seen from garden.

57. Hadassah Medical Cente
rior detail (opposite page).

58. Hadassah Medical Center. Visitors' waiting room seen from exterior.

59. Hadassah Medical Center. Nurse's school.

60. Hadassah Medical Center. Exterior detail.

61. Hadassah Medical Center. Chapel balcony.

62. Hadassah Medical Center. Chapel balcony seen from terrace.

63. Anglo-Palestine Bank. Exterior detail.

64. Anglo-Palestine Bank, Jerusalem, 1937-38.

65. Anglo-Palestine Bank. Interior detail (opposite page).

67. Government Hospital, Haifa, 1936-38. Main entrance court.

66. Government Hospital. Exterior detail.

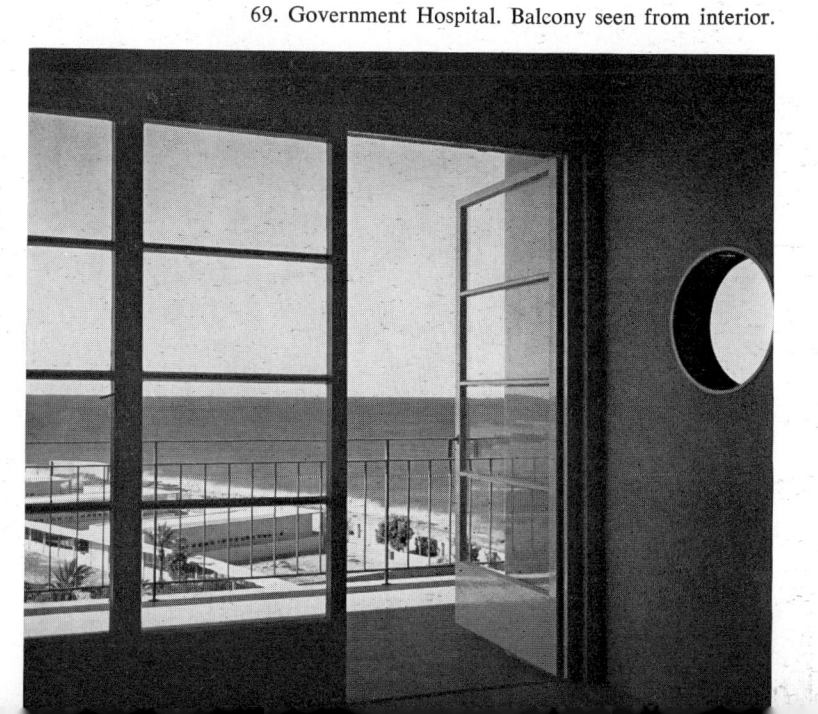

68. Government Hospital. Exterior detail.

69. Government Hospital. Balcony seen from interior.

70. Agricultural College. Exterior detail.

71. Agricultural College. Entrance court.

72. Agricultural College, Rehoboth, 1939.

73. Maimonides Hospital. Exterior detail.

74. Maimonides Hospital, San Francisco, 1946-50 (opposite page

75. Russell House, San Francisco, 1950-51.

76. Russell House. Exterior detail.

77. Russell House. Interior.

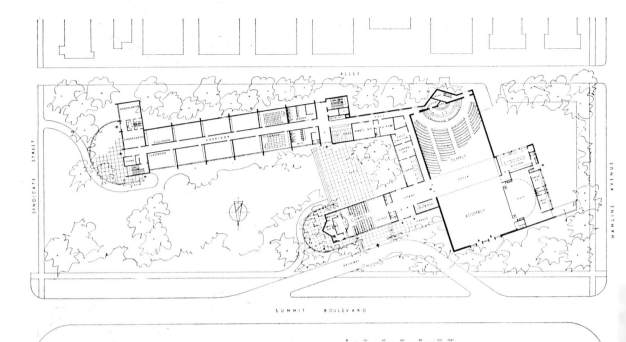

78. Mount Zion Temple and Community Center, St. Paul, 1950-54. Plan.

79. Synagogue and Community Center, Cleveland, 1946-52. Plan.

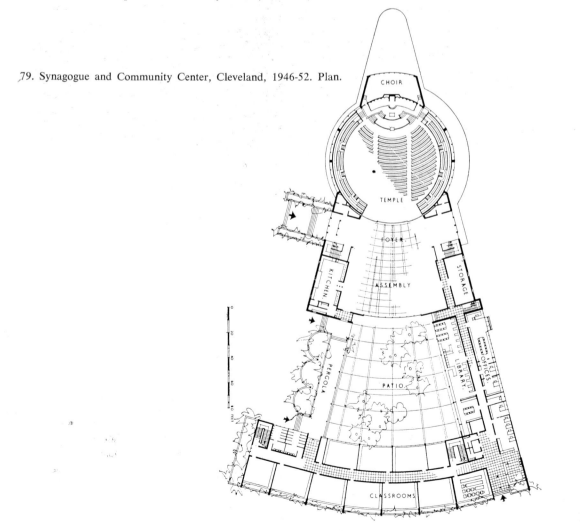

80. B'nai Amoona Synagogue and Community Center, St. Louis, 1946-50.

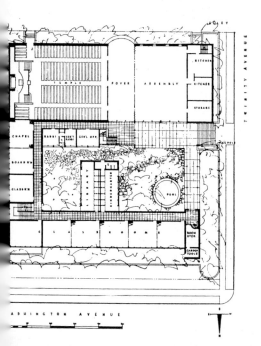

81. B'nai Amoona, St. Louis. Plan.

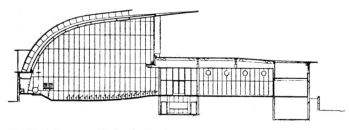

82. B'nai Amoona, St. Louis. Section.

83. B'nai Amoona, St. Louis. Interior.

84. B'nai Amoona, St. Louis. Interior detail.

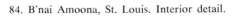

85. Synagogue and Community Center, Cleveland, 1946-52.

87. Cleveland Synagogue and Community Center. Interior of chapel.

88. Cleveland Synagogue and Community Center. Detail.

. Cleveland Synagogue and Community Center. Interior (opposite ge).

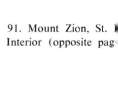

89. Mount Zion Temple and Community Center, St. Paul, 1950-54.

90. Mount Zion, St. Paul. Model, first design.

92. Temple Emanu-El. Interior, temple and assembly hall combined.

93. Emanu-El, Grand Rapids, Michigan, 1953

94. Emanu-El, Grand Rapids. Temple interior.

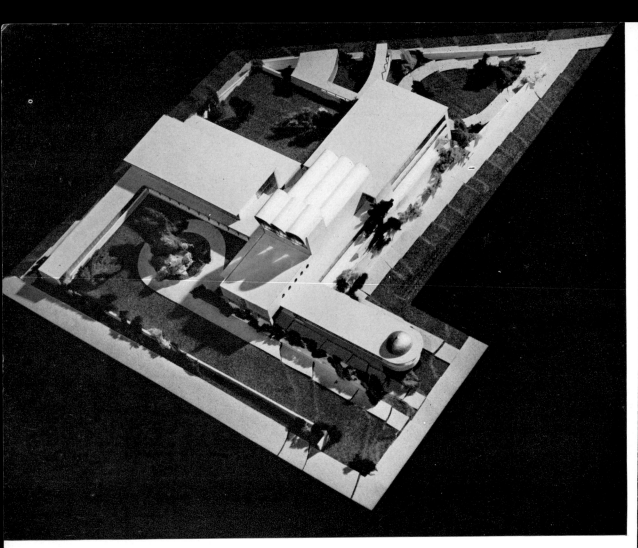

95. Beth-El Temple and Community Center, Baltimore, 1948. Model. (*not executed*)

96. Beth-El, Baltimore. Model.

97. Beth-El, Baltimore. Sketch for interior.

98. Beth-El, Baltimore. Sketch for exterior.

99. Emanu-El Temple and Community Center, Dallas, Texas, 1951. Model. (*not executed*)

100. Temple and Community Center, Washington, D. C., 1948. Model. (*not executed*)

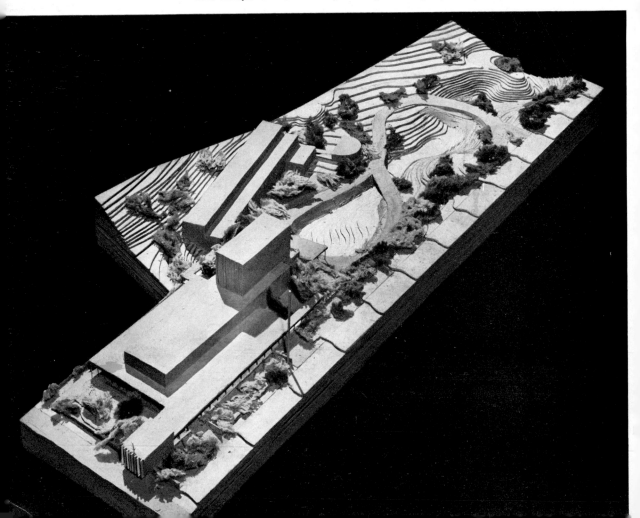

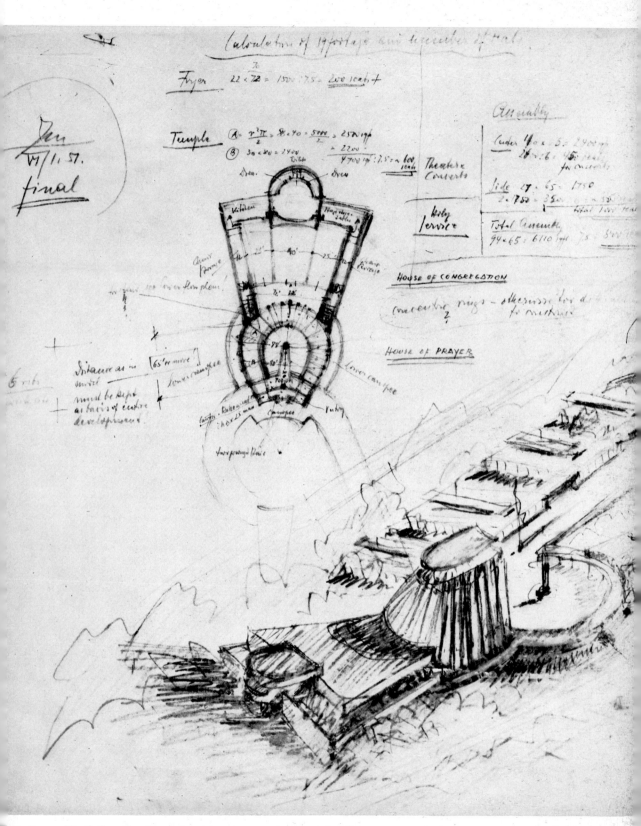

101. Emanu-El, Dallas. Sketches.

102. Memorial for Six Million Jewish Victims of the Nazis, Riverside Park, New York, 1951. First design. (*not executed*)

103. Memorial for Six Million Jewish Victims of the Nazis. Second design. (*not executed*)

NOTES

1. Henry-Russell Hitchcock, *Architecture—Nineteenth and Twentieth Centuries,* Penguin Books, Baltimore, Md., 1958, p. 364.

2. Eric Mendelsohn said this in a lecture, *My Own Contribution to the Development of Contemporary Architecture,* at the University of Los Angeles School of Architecture, March 17, 1948.

3. *Ibid.*

4. *Ibid.*

5. *Ibid.*

6. From a memorial essay on Eric Mendelsohn by Hans J. Schiller which was quoted at length in *Architectural Forum,* February, 1955.

7. From a letter Mendelsohn wrote to his wife, in 1919, which he quoted in his lecture *My Own Contribution to the Development of Contemporary Architecture.*

8. Mendelsohn's lecture to the University of California School of Architecture, April 2, 1953.

9. At this writing none of these buildings have been completed except some of Candela's. Sketches and models have been widely published, however. See, for instance, "Architecture and Imagery—Four New Buildings," *Museum of Modern Art Bulletin,* Vol. 26, No. 2, New York, 1959.

10. Lecture, *My Own Contribution to the Development of Contemporary Architecture.*

11. S. Giedion, *Space, Time and Architecture—The Growth of a New Tradition,* Harvard University Press, Cambridge, 1942, pp. 350-432.

12. The letter is dated November 13, 1941.

13. Quoted by Arnold Whittick, *Eric Mendelsohn,* F. W. Dodge, New York, 1956, p. 41.

14. Quoted by Whittick, *op. cit.,* p. 204.

15. In one of his many letters to Mrs. Mendelsohn, written after her husband's death, van de Velde calls Mendelsohn "one of his most faithful and fervent pupils." Mendelsohn often referred to van de Velde's work as "the first accomplished fact of a creative resurgence in architecture." This influence is entirely omitted by writers like Whittick or Joedicke. The common contention seems to be that, as Joedicke puts it, "of the architects who had an appreciable influence in determining the path of modern architecture, Eric Mendelsohn was most lastingly affected by

Expressionism." (Jürgen Joedicke, *A History of Modern Architecture,* transl. from the German, Praeger, New York, 1959, p. 65.)

16. Whittick, *op. cit.,* p. 65.

17. Le Corbusier makes no bones about the fact that the shell of his Notre Dame du Haut at Ronchamp "will lie on walls made of the salvaged stones" of the former, destroyed chapel. (Cf. Le Corbusier, *The Chapel at Ronchamp,* Praeger, New York, 1957, p. 90.)

18. Cf. "A Top Architect's Hospital," *Architectural Forum,* February, 1951.

19. Quoted from reminiscences Richard Neutra was kind enough to write for this book at the request of the author. The account of Mendelsohn's first meeting with Frank Lloyd Wright is also based on Neutra's charming recollections.

20. Mendelsohn recalled this remark in his lecture *My Own Contribution to the Development of Contemporary Architecture.*

21. Quoted from a personal letter by Professor Werner M. Moser, of the *Technische Hochschule* in Zürich, Switzerland, to Mrs. Mendelsohn, dated December 21, 1959, and translated from the original German by the author.

22. Another design in which the two halls for the Palace of the Soviets are combined in one building is that by Walter Gropius, who placed them into one large, circular building. All major submissions in this competition are illustrated in the May, 1932, issue of *Architectural Review.*

23. Jürgen Joedicke, *op. cit.,* p. 127.

24. This, to the best of the author's recollection, is the gist of Mies's answer to a question on the validity of regional architecture asked in the course of a press conference during the 1960 convention of The American Institute of Architects at San Francisco, where Mies received the AIA Gold Medal.

25. Quoted in *Religious Buildings of Today,* edited by John Knox Shear, F. W. Dodge, New York, 1957, p. 4.

26. Quoted by Whittick, *op. cit.,* p. 173.

27. As quoted by Mendelsohn in his lecture *My Own Contribution to the Development of Contemporary Architecture.*

28. Quoted by Whittick, *op. cit.,* p. 160.

29. Proceedings of the Second National Conference and Exhibit of Synagogue Architecture and Art, sponsored by the Union of American Hebrew Congregations, New York, 1958.

30. In a letter to Mrs. Mendelsohn, dated October 1, 1953, van de Velde wrote that in Mendelsohn's death he deplores the loss *"d'un génie qui est frappé au moment même où il disposait du maximum des moyens pour l'empreinte définitive du style du XXᵉ siècle."*

SELECTED CHRONOLOGICAL LIST OF
BUILDINGS AND PROJECTS

1919   Einstein Tower (completed 1924)
Hall for a hat factory in Luckenwalde (Steinberg, Herman & Co.)

1920   Additional buildings for the Luckenwalde hat factory

1921   Wins competition for an office building on Kemperplatz, Berlin
Addition to *Berliner Tageblatt* building

1922   Semidetached houses in Berlin Charlottenburg
Silk store in Gleiwitz

1923   Visits Palestine to design hydroelectric power stations (*not executed*)
Wins competition (with Richard Neutra) for a business center in Haifa
(*not executed*)
Villa Sternefeld on Heerstrasse, Berlin

1924   Herpich men's store, Leipzigerstrasse, Berlin

1925   Manufacturing plant for the Leningrad Textile Trust, U.S.S.R.

1926   Department stores for Schocken in Nuremberg and Stuttgart and for Petersdorff in Breslau
Jewish cemetery in Königsberg
Several shops, showrooms, and office buildings in Berlin

1927   Mosse Pavilion for the Press Exhibition at Cologne
Universum movie theater and other buildings for the Woga development project on Kurfürstendamm, Berlin

1928   Schocken department store, Stuttgart
Metal Workers' Union Building, Berlin
Enters international competition for the Palace of the Soviets, Moscow

1929   Columbus House and redevelopment scheme for Potsdamerplatz, Berlin

1930   Mendelsohn's own residence, "Am Rupenhorn," Berlin
Jewish Youth Center, Essen
First prize in competition for Cathedral Square, Magdeburg (*not executed*)

1931   Zinc plant in Magdeburg (*not executed*)
       Designs redevelopment scheme for Alexanderplatz, Berlin (*not executed*)
       Wins first prize for the headquarters building of the Berlin Transit Company (*not executed*)

1933   Nimmo residence in Buckinghamshire, England
       Wins competition, builds De La Warr Pavilion, Bexhill (with Chermayeff)

1934   Is invited to Palestine to design the residence of Chaim Weizmann in Rehoboth, near Tel Aviv

1935   Residence and a library for Salman Schocken, Jerusalem

1936   Plans for Hebrew University on Mount Scopus, Jerusalem
       Hadassah University Medical Center, Mount Scopus
       Government Hospital, Haifa

1937   Anglo-Palestine Bank, Jerusalem
       Trade School, Yagour
       Hotel and business center, Haifa (*not executed*)

1939   Daniel Wolf Research Laboratories, Rehoboth
       Agricultural College, Rehoboth

1941   Mendelsohn exhibition at the Museum of Modern Art, New York

1946   Maimonides Hospital, San Francisco (completed 1950)
       Synagogue and Community Center for the Congregation B'nai Amoona, St. Louis (completed 1950)
       Synagogue and Community Center for the Hebrew Congregation in Cleveland, Ohio (completed 1952)

1948   Synagogue and Community Center for Hebrew Congregation, Washington, D.C. (*not executed*)
       Synagogue and Community Center for Beth El Congregation, Baltimore, Md. (only school was built)
       Synagogue and Community Center for Congregation Emanu-El, Grand Rapids, Michigan (completed 1952)

1950   Residence for Mr. and Mrs. Leon Russell, San Francisco
       Electronic Research and Development Plant, Palo Alto, California
       Synagogue and Community Center for Mount Zion Hebrew Congregation, St. Paul, Minnesota (completed 1954)

1951   Synagogue and Community Center for Congregation Emanu-El, Dallas, Texas (*not executed*)
       Laboratories for the Atomic Energy Commission, Berkeley, California (completed 1953)
       Memorials to the Jewish victims of the Nazis, Riverside Park, New York (*not executed*)

CHRONOLOGY

1887   Born in Allenstein, East Prussia, one of the five children of a business-man

1907   Studies economics at the University of Munich

1908   Enters *Technische Hochschule* at Berlin to study architecture and engineering

1909   Transfers to *Technische Hochschule* in Munich, where he meets *Blaue Reiter* group of painters and other expressionists

1912   Graduates from architecture school and opens practice in Munich

1915   Marries Louise Maas. First sketches of his architectural "visions"

1917   Is drafted into war service on the Russian and later the Western front. More sketches

1919   Returns from the war, opens office in Berlin and exhibits his wartime sketches — "Architecture in Steel and Concrete" — at the Cassirer art gallery in Berlin
Is invited to Holland for lecture tour

1921   Loss of one eye due to cancer

1923   Second lecture tour in Holland

1924   Visits the United States and meets Frank Lloyd Wright at his home, Taliesin, in Spring Green, Wisconsin

1925   Makes several trips to the Soviet Union

1932   Is elected member of the Prussian Academy of Arts

1933   Hitler becomes German chancellor and the Mendelsohns emigrate to Holland (where he plans a European Academy of Art) and later to England
Opens architectural practice with Serge Chermayeff

1934   Begins series of architectural commissions in Palestine

1941   Leaves Palestine for the United States

1942   Guggenheim Fellowship. Extensive travels through the U. S. and lectures at Michigan, Columbia, Princeton, Cornell, Harvard, Yale, and other universities. Consultant to the U. S. War Department

1945   Opens architectural practice in San Francisco in a short-lived partnership with John Elsin Dinwiddie and Albert Henry Hill. Teaches at the University of California School of Architecture

1953   Dies September 15.

SELECTED BIBLIOGRAPHY OF BOOKS AND ARTICLES WRITTEN BY ERIC MENDELSOHN

Amerika: Bilderbuch eines Architekten, R. Mosse, Berlin, 1926.

Russland, Europa, Amerika—ein architektonischer Querschnitt, R. Mosse, Berlin, 1929, 214 pp.

Erich Mendelsohn, Das Gesamtschaffen des Architekten, R. Mosse, Berlin, 1930, 252 pp.

Der Schöpferische Sinn der Krise, lecture given in Zürich, May, 1932, B. Cassirer, Berlin, 1932, 29 pp.

"Das Columbushaus in Berlin," *Monatshefte für Baukunst und Städtebau* Heft 2, pp. 81-88, February, 1933.

Palestine and the World of Tomorrow, Jerusalem Press Ltd., Jerusalem, 1940, 19 pp.

Three Lectures on Architecture, University of California Press, Berkeley and Los Angeles, 1944, 48 pp.

SELECTED BIBLIOGRAPHY ON
ERIC MENDELSOHN

BOOKS

Guido Lodovico Luzzatto, *Erich Mendelsohn,* Estratto da *La Rassegna Mensile di Israel,* Citta di Castello, 1932, 42 pp.

Structures and Sketches, with an introduction by Mendelsohn, translated from the German by Herman George Scheffauer, E. Benn, Ltd., London, 1924, 66 pp.

Mario Federico Roggero, *Il Contributo di Mendelsohn alla Evolutione dell'architettura moderna,* Libreria Editrice Politecnica Tamburini, Milan, 1952, 154 pp.

Arnold Whittick, *Eric Mendelsohn,* F. W. Dodge, New York, 1956, 219 pp.

ARTICLES

Karl Konrad Düssel, "Drei Kaufhäuser Schocken in Nürnberg Stuttgart und Chemnitz von Erich Mendelsohn," *Moderne Bauformen,* Heft 11, 1930.

"Leisure at the Seaside. IV. The Architect," *Architectural Review,* July, 1936, pp. 19-28.

"House at Rehoboth, Palestine," *Architectural Review,* October, 1937, pp. 123-25.

"Current Architecture: HOSPITALS," *Architectural Review,* February, 1939, pp. 83-86.

"Bank Building at Jerusalem," *Architectural Review,* June, 1941, pp. 119-22.

"Agricultural College," *Architectural Review,* September, 1941, pp. 77-78.

"Eric Mendelsohn," *Architectural Forum,* May, 1947, pp. 73-77.

"A Top Architect's Hospital," *Architectural Forum,* February, 1951, pp. 92-99.

"Erich Mendelsohn," *Architectural Forum,* April, 1953, pp. 105-21.

"The Last Work of a Great Architect," *Architectural Forum,* February, 1955.

"Eric Mendelsohn," by Irving D. Shapiro, *Journal of the AIA,* June, 1958.

INDEX

Numbers in regular roman type refer to text pages; *italic* figures refer to the plates.

SOURCES OF ILLUSTRATION

Alfred Bernheim, Jerusalem: 59, 60, 62, 69, 71, 72
Herbert Felton, London: 43, 44, 45, 46
I. Kalter, Tel Aviv: 49, 50, 53
Arthur Köster, Berlin: 20, 24, 25, 27, 32, 33, 36, 41
Mas, Barcelona: 3
Neumann-Rabe: 34
Hans Schiller, San Francisco: 73, 76, 77, 80, 83, 84, 85, 86, 88, 89, 91, 92, 94
Schleissner, Rehoboth: 51
Dean Stone—Hugo Steccati, San Francisco: 74, 90, 95, 96, 99, 102, 103